Work From Home

Jobs Ideas, Companies, And Passive Income Opportunities To Make Money Online And Get 6 Figure Income And The Lifestyle You Dream Of

Introduction

I want to thank you and congratulate you for purchasing the book, "Work From Home: Jobs Ideas, Companies, And Passive Income Opportunities To Make Money Online And Get 6 Figure Income And The Lifestyle You Dream Of."This is a how-to guide.

In it, we shall be looking at the various online job ideas, companies, and businesses you can start today and in so doing, get started on the path to earning a 6-figure passive income and the financial freedom you strive towards as you seek out the lifestyle of your dreams.

You are here because you want to learn how to work from home so that you can have more control over how you use your time, your income, and the lifestyle you live. The good news is that you can do just that.

Thanks to technological advancements, no matter who you are, you can work online and generate six figures from the comfort of your home or from any location/setting of your choice because to make money online, all you truly need is a computer or laptop, a working, stable internet connection, and knowledge of what to do.

From these basic things, **a computer**—modern smartphones or tablets count—and **a basic, but preferably fast internet connection**, things that are now readily available to many of us, you can comfortably get started with working online from home and striving towards achieving the financial freedom and independence you deserve so that you can create the lifestyle of your dreams.

This book covers the knowledge part of the equation.

From it, you are going to derive practical skills and strategies you can use to get started on your quest to make money online and from any location using various ideas that you can implement full time or part time depending on your present financial situation and time commitments, among many other fabulous ideas, we shall:

Discuss how to go from being in a financial pinch, or in a job you hate, to using online job ideas and companies that give you more control over how you use your time to earn money, and allow you to earn enough to quit your lousy day job!

Various online business ideas you can start implementing right now, and others that, depending on how you implement them, have the potential to become passive income streams, i.e., online businesses that generate income passively, without much time demand. We shall cover ideas such as freelancing/trading your skills for income, blogging, creating online businesses such as drop shipping, blogs, affiliate marketing, etc.

We shall also outline a systematic set of instructions you can use to implement the various ideas as soon as you commit to the pursuit of a 6-figure income and the lifestyle you dream of, a lifestyle that allows you complete financial and time freedom. The essence of this guide is to give you hands-on knowledge you can start using right now!

Thanks again for purchasing this book. I hope you enjoy it!

Get FREE ebooks before they are published

We have a reviewers list which we send our books for free before being published.
They enjoy the ebook beforehand, we only expect to get an honest review from the in return. **Join Here**

Affiliate Links Disclosure

Dear reader, note that some of the links in this post are affiliate links and if you go through them to make a purchase I will earn a commission. Note I link these companies and their products because of their quality and the value they can provide as additional resources to this book and not because of the commission I receive from your purchases. The decision is yours, and whether or not you decide to buy something is completely up to you. To help you identify which of the links on the books are related to an affiliate program an (*) sign is included in all of them.

© Copyright 2019 by Digital Media Life - All rights reserved

This document is geared towards providing exact and reliable information in regards to the topic and issue covered. The publication is sold with the idea that the publisher is not required to render accounting, officially permitted, or otherwise, qualified services. If advice is necessary, legal or professional, a practiced individual in the profession should be ordered.

- From a Declaration of Principles which was accepted and approved equally by a Committee of the American Bar Association and a Committee of Publishers and Associations.

In no way is it legal to reproduce, duplicate, or transmit any part of this document in either electronic means or in printed format. Recording of this publication is strictly prohibited and any storage of this document is not allowed unless with written permission from the publisher. All rights reserved.

The information provided herein is stated to be truthful and consistent, in that any liability, in terms of inattention or otherwise, by any usage or abuse of any policies, processes, or directions contained within is the solitary and utter responsibility of the recipient reader. Under no circumstances will any legal responsibility or blame be held against the publisher for any reparation, damages, or monetary loss due to the information herein, either directly or indirectly.

Respective authors own all copyrights not held by the publisher.

The information herein is offered for informational purposes solely, and is universal as so. The presentation of the information is without contract or any type of guarantee assurance.
The trademarks that are used are without any consent, and the publication of the trademark is without permission or backing by the trademark owner. All trademarks and brands within this book are for clarifying purposes only and are the owned by the owners themselves, not affiliated with this document.

Table of Contents

Work From Home

Introduction

Table of Contents

Chapter 1: Online Job Ideas To Get You Started Right AWAY!

Freelancing/Gig Economy

   Freelancing Ideas and Tips to Get You Started

      Step 1

      Step 2

Chapter 2: Sell Products Online

   Steps and Ideas to Get You Started With Selling Products Online

      Step 1

      Step 2

   Tips for Selling on Amazon

   Tips for Selling on eBay

   Tips for Snelling Online with Drop shipping

Chapter 3: Online Business That Generate a 6-Figure, Passive Income

Blogging

   Blogging For Income: A Quick Getting Started Guide

      Step 1

      Step 2

      Step 3

Step 4

Blogging Success Tips

A Basic Introduction to Affiliate Marketing

A Brief Introduction to Selling Informational Products

Conclusion

Bonus:Get our next books FREE

Chapter 1: Online Job Ideas To Get You Started Right AWAY!

NOTE: This chapter of the guide assumes you are unhappy with your present means of generating income. Out of this assumption, the chapter notes that because of this discontent, you have decided to look into work from home job opportunities and companies that give you more control over how you make money online from one month to the next.

Now that we have that out of the way:

When implemented as discussed here, the following job ideas and companies have the potential to help you get started with generating income from home right away or in the next several days.

Freelancing/Gig Economy

Freelancing, sometimes called the gig economy, is one of the fastest ways to get started with work from home opportunities, making money online, and generating 6-figure passive income. One of the most amazing things about freelancing is its broadness.

By definition, freelancing is *"offering services or skills to various businesses or companies without necessarily being part of the daily, internal operations of the business or company."*

Because as a freelancer, you are free to offer your services or skills to as many businesses or companies as you would want, or to take up different kinds of freelancing opportunities (even simultaneously), you become somewhat *self-employed*. This is in the sense that even though you collaborate with various businesses and from these collaborations, generate income, you control how you work, when you work and for how long you work depending on a remote-worker contract. You also control from where you work, when you receive payments, as well as how much you generate in income from one month to the next.

If you want to get started working for yourself from home as fast as possible, freelancing is the way to go because in addition to allowing you time freedom, depending on the kinds of services you offer or skills you have in your repertoire, it can also allow you to start generating 6-figures (or more) quickly. Here are examples.

Examples

If you have great organizational skills and you know your way around a computer, scheduling meetings, etc., you can freelance as a virtual assistant—virtual assistants earn an average of $16 per hour. If you have access to a computer, have a good ear for spoken language, are a fast typist, and you have some free time, perhaps 3-4 hours in the evening after a day job, you can take up transcription jobs—transcribers earn $15-$30 per hour.

Freelancing is varied; your approach towards it is what matters because it depends on your skills or service set. If you have web design/developer skills, you can market these skills as a freelancer and sell them to willing buyers, companies, or business for a consistent income each month—freelance web developer/designers generate $51,000-$76,000 annually.

If you know your way around social media marketing for business, you can freelance as a social media manager or marketer; social media managers/marketers generate an average of $49,881 annually.

The broadness of freelancing makes it so that anyone interested in generating an income from home can do so by capitalizing on available skills, services, and resources.

Because we cannot cover every freelancing idea conceivable—there are too many—what we are going to do in this guide is outline simple ideas and strategies you can use to get started with freelancing immediately.

Freelancing Ideas and Tips to Get You Started

Let us make this systematic.

Step 1

To start freelancing, the first thing you need to do is take stock of your skillset or to think about which valuable services you can offer the open market in general using gig economy technologies, or to specific businesses you know could benefit from your skills or expertise in a specific field.

As mentioned, your skills and interest dictate what kind of freelancer you become. You can become a freelancing virtual assistant, digital marketer, translator, web designer, content writer, transcriber, photographer, voiceover artist, animator, customer or service assistant; if you can name the job, you can probably 'freelance' it.

Give this some serious thought but do not overthink it especially if your desire is to start making money online as fast as possible. Just choose a skill you think is valuable and get rolling. The most important thing to making a consistent income while working at home is to get started, you can always add up or change your business model later on.

Think about your schedule too. Do you want to work from home part or full time? Work from home job opportunities are flexible but in the end, you still have to plan your time well to ensure that once clients or businesses remote-contract you, you have time scheduled to fulfil your end of the bargain depending on the services or skills you are offering.

You can use freelancing as a source of extra income, meaning doing it part time to cultivate a second stream of income beyond your day job. This is a great way to get started. By committing to it part-time, your freelancing income can grow to a point where it eventually surpasses the income generated from your day job, thus allowing you time freedom, the ability to quit your day job, and to start creating the lifestyle you dream of, one not constrained by the shackles of a 9-5 job.

You can also dive in head first, full-time, which is especially good if you have a valuable set of skills or if you would like to start working from home or independently as fast as possible.

If you are unsure of which freelancing services/skills to offer, look over the invaluable resources below and use what you learn to create a general list of freelance services you can offer.

This is one of the main sites to offer your services and get some ideas and pricing Fiverr*.

Step 2

After deciding which freelance field you would like to pursue, the next step is to search online for platforms used by freelancers in your field of choice. Here, we shall use a simple example.

Assume that after taking stock of your available skills and time commitment, you decide you can offer copy or blog writing skills to businesses in the tech industry. Or that after taking stock, you realize you can spend 2+ hours transcribing, taking customer calls, managing a social media page or campaign, managing a website, etc., you can use gig economy platforms such as Fiverr, UpWork, Behance, FlexJobs, Gigster, TaskRabbit, and other such sites to find clients or businesses looking for someone offering the skills you have on offer. It is that simple really!.

Personally I have used most of them but found Fiverr* the easier and more reliable to use.

Freelancing is a great job idea that you can use to replace a traditional income, have complete control over your work lifestyle, and because it is scalable, it has the potential to become a passive business that helps you generate a steady income month after month.

Now that you have an idea of how you can get started with freelancing, use the following tips that make it easier to market your freelancing business well to ensure it scales and generates the income you want.

Market yourself

As a freelancer, you are a business, a brand. Therefore, you have to market yourself and do so well because, if you fail to advertise your business, you will soon advertise it for sale, or you will not generate the income you strive to generate.

Think of yourself as a business; what is your unique selling point? What do you have to offer? Make sure you market yourself in a way that allows you to illustrate how what you have to offer benefits the business that would want to hire you. An invaluable marketing tip is to ensure you have a visible online presence. Have a blog, visible social media pages, and any other visibility-signal you may want to have in place depending on the type of freelancing skill you would like to offer. Have in place an effective marketing strategy too and a way to display your portfolio or skills to potential business collaborators; this shall help you scale and grow your business.

If you are using a gig economy website or platform, make sure your profile is promising to potential collaborators; remember that with freelancing, the effectiveness of how you market yourself will largely determine your income potential and ability to scale the business.

Network like your business depends on it because it does

Your professional collaborations will become a large part of your social and work life as a freelancer. From the moment, you decide to get into a specific field as a freelancer, connect and network like your business depends on it because as implied, it does.

For freelancers, networking is an invaluable part of marketing and branding. Aim to have an on-going list of clients, colleagues, businesses you can work with, potential clients, other great freelancers in your field, mentors, etc.

Join social groups visited by other freelancers in your field as well as groups patronized by your dream clients—Twitter, Facebook, LinkedIn, and other popular social sites will prove invaluable here.

The more effectively you network and collaborate with other businesses and freelancers within and outside your field, the easier it will be to scale your business. This brings us to the next tip.

Outsource and systemize

As you continue marketing yourself well and delivering to clients the value you promise, your business will grow multi-fold but especially from word of mouth marketing and recommendations from happy clients or businesses.

As your business grows, scale by outsourcing some of the work. For instance, if you market your copywriting skills well and get a steady stream of copywriting work, scale your business by outsourcing some of the work to other capable freelancers you have networked with socially.

Outsourcing is a great way to grow and scale a freelancing business fast. It allows you time freedom and in instances where you are outsourcing paid-client work to capable freelancers, you can earn a service arbitrage fee that allows you to earn more than you would normally earn if you were a one-person operation. For instance, if you have tons of writing work billed at $200 per article, you can outsource some of the work to other capable freelancers within your field for as much as a 45% arbitrage fee ($90 as profit per article). If you outsource 3 articles every day of the month, the arbitrage fee adds up to $8,100 per month.

As you can see from the simple example above, outsourcing is a great way to get you working on your freelance business instead of working in it, a very important distinction.

Systematisation, on the other hand, is automating your service offerings and other tasks that you can automate or pre-schedule, so that you can have more time to dedicate to the growth of the business into a steady income business, you need to use all available tools: auto responders, schedulers, and the likes. Tools like [Aweber*](Aweber) can help you with setting up your system, creating mailing campaigns etc.

Have in place a funnel, a system that allows you to capture and nature leads for your business; for example, if you start a freelance photography business, have in place an automatic booking system that allows potential clients to book you.

If you can automate an aspect of your freelance business, do so because it will free up your time and significantly influence your ability to scale the business into one that generates a 6-figure passive income month-to-month.

If freelancing is not your cup of tea, you can:

Chapter 2: Sell Products Online

Selling products (or stuff) online is another great business model you can use to create a work from home business.

This business model allows you to operate an online retail store, which as you can imagine, has the potential to become a massively successful business. Selling products online is such an effective business model that when done right, it has the potential to generate upwards of $10,000 in passive income each month.

One of the advantages of this business model is that the work involved is not as monumental as one would imagine; this is primarily because you can approach selling products from various angles.

The simplest way to go about it is to visit garage sales or flea markets on the weekends and buy physical products that you can sell online for a profit on platforms such as eBay, Amazon, Craigslist, Etsy, or the various other online retailers that allow third party sellers. This approach is a fast and effective way to start a work from home online store that has the potential to turn into a steady income stream that is profitable and fun to maintain.

Another simple way to go about it is to create your own products and sell them online either on your own store or using any of the aforementioned online retailers that give third party sellers the ability to have an online storefront.

Another way to go about it, and this is perhaps the most popular and most profitable/scalable way to go about it, is to buy products at wholesale prices, stock them, market them, and ship them out whenever you get an order.

You can alternatively employ the drop shipping method where you go into legally binding contracts with businesses and companies that stock your products in their warehouses or production plants, and process sale orders by shipping them to customers.

Steps and Ideas to Get You Started With Selling Products Online

Here is how to get started with this work from home opportunity that has massive potential:

Step 1

The first thing you need to do is pick the right products to sell. Luckily, you can sell just about anything; ideally though, you want to aim for a product that is both popular throughout the year (an evergreen product) and one that has good returns.

A great product is one that solves a problem, one that inspires passion—in you and others—or one that has branding potential or the ability to become a popularly bought item (viral).

Market research will prove invaluable here; it will allow you to know whom you are selling to, which will prove invaluable when it comes to marketing your online products/business.

Step 2

Now that you have a great product to sell, you can sell it through your own store, through social media, or through the various other platforms mentioned earlier—eBay, Amazon, Etsy, etc. Choose a platform that matches your needs or if none does, create your own e-commerce store or site, which is now easier than it has ever been.

On the question of whether to create your store from scratch or to use a hosted store such as Shopify, WooCommerce, etc., the main thing to keep in mind is visibility: choose a platform that is visible and that allows you to reach your target audience as effectively as possible. With this business model, the more effectively you serve a specific segment of the market (called a niche), the likelier the success of your online retail store or business. This goes back to positioning and marketing your business effectively.

Now that you know how to start implementing this business model, here are various strategies guaranteed to help you sell online effectively and profitably on various platforms:

Tips for Selling on Amazon

Amazon in a great way to get started with selling products online fast. As shall be the case with all other platforms we shall discuss briefly in this guide, with Amazon, the secret to success is choosing a great product.

To list your products on Amazon, you can pay $0.99 for individual listings, or go for an unlimited license (costs $39.99/month) that gives you the ability to make as many postings as you want depending on the product you intend to sell.

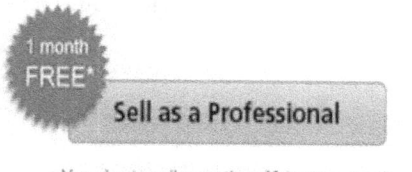

Sell as a Professional	Sell as an Individual
You plan to sell more than 40 items a month	You plan to sell fewer than 40 items a month
Unlimited sales for $39.99 a month + other selling fees	$0.99 per sale + other selling fees
What can I sell as a professional?	What can I sell as an individual?

The individual plan is cost friendly to someone just getting started with this business model. As your business grows and you sell more products, you can invest in the unlimited license.

Another important thing to note is that Amazon is also a search engine; this means that if you use the right keywords to describe your products, Amazon will drive traffic to your products by listing them as the most relevant for specific user-entered keywords. Invest some time into learning about general SEO strategies and SEO strategies specific to selling on Amazon. The following resource pages should get you started with SEO for Amazon—and other forms of online businesses—but try to learn about SEO from many other sources.

To scale your Amazon business, after learning how to use the platform and selling several products successfully, consider investing in Amazon ads.

Tips for Selling on eBay

EBay is still one of the best places to sell online; the platform receives more than a ¼ of a billion searches every month and is one of the most successful online retailers.

In addition to keeping in mind the tips mentioned above, also note that to achieve success with eBay, your listing should have impeccable pictures, and that the more traffic you drive to your listings, the faster you can generate an income from this business model and scale the business; clear pictures will elevate your listing tenfold.

Be mindful of how you describe your products too. This goes back to the need to learn more about SEO so that in addition to optimizing your product description with keywords, you can also describe individual products in a way that triggers a conversion, the term we use to describe potential audiences turning into actual buyers and eventual brand ambassadors.

Running an eBay store is relatively easy because the platform is very intuitive in the sense that it gives its sellers access to a wide range of tools that make managing various elements of the business such as choosing an ideal shipping option, calculating postage, and package-tracking information relatively easy.

You can learn more about selling with eBay from the following resource page: EBay resources.

Tips for Snelling Online with Drop shipping

Drop shipping allows you to operate a successful online retail business without ever having to deal with the hassle of stocking your merchandise at physical warehouses or handling the shipping elements of the business.

In this business model, you get into agreements with suppliers and manufacturers who agree to fulfil all your orders; in this sense, you do not have to worry about handling and shipping. All you have to concentrate on is marketing your business and the products you have chosen to sell online and whenever you get an order, you simply forward the order to the supplier or manufacturer who then 'fulfils' it by shipping it to the customer. Drop shipping is easy to start—you can start with as little as $100—and easy to scale too, if you implement the right strategies.

To achieve drop-shipping success, choose products, suppliers, and manufacturers wisely. Work with reputable drop shipping businesses and only sell products you have researched and determined that they will resonate well with your intended target audience.

In addition, since you will not be personally handling the physical products during the dispatch and shipping process, you must have in place an effective customer service system that allows you to handle orders, follow ups, confirmations, complaints, and returns effectively. Offering excellent customer support will yield tons of benefits one of which is that it will help you create a valued and respected business or brand that has a loyal following and mouth-to-mouth advocates/marketers who recommend your business because it provides value.

NOTE: With all forms of online jobs and businesses, value is the keyword that will determine your income potential. The more value you provide to a specific segment of the market, the more valuable your business is likely to be long-term.

With drop shipping—and with most of the other selling online platforms we have discussed here—you especially want to very mindful of how you handle returns, complaints, or follow-ups. Always aim to replace returned items; where that is not possible, ensure you give customers refunds as illustrated in your returns-policy. At the minimum, clearly define how customers can return including where they should send the returned package. Should they send it to you or to the vendor? Who shall handle the cost of shipping the returned item? A clearly created, effective marketing and customer support plan should help you iron most of these things.

As is the case with freelancing, with selling online, you also want to strive towards automation as the business grows and scales into one that generates a 6-figure passive income.

With this business model, you want automate email collection, social media marketing, Paid Per Click (PPC) ads on all platforms including social media and Google ads, email marketing, publishing blog content, etc.

Automating is what will allow you to get to a point where you can run your online store in as little as an hour or two a day. The process to this point takes time but if you diligently market your business, selling online is one of the best ways to create an online business that generates thousands of dollars in passive income each month.

With this business model, and with all the other business models mentioned in this guide, how effectively you market yourself will significantly influence the income you generate from one month to the next. Employ as many, effectual marketing strategies as you can.

As you learn more about online businesses, aim to learn more about using PPC ads offered by the various social and dedicated advertising platforms. Aim to create effective leads and sales funnel that work to drive a consistent flow of traffic to your landing pages, product pages, and all other pages that help you nurture leads into customers.

Chapter 3: Online Business That Generate a 6-Figure, Passive Income

Unlike the ideas discussed in the last section of the guide, the work-from-home jobs and business ideas we shall discuss in this section have massive passive income potential.

Ideas such as affiliate marketing, blogging, and selling informational products, the main ideas we shall focus on in this section of the guide, may start out active in the sense that you have to dedicate time and energy. However, if you implement these ideas as illustrated here, they have great potential to generate a substantial income with very little upkeep.

Blogging

We start with blogging because upon mastering the most important blogging elements, you will be in a position to implement the other two ideas with a degree of ease and idea implementation efficiency.

Blogging for passive income is relatively straightforward. The main things you need to do are create a blog, which is relatively easy, curate web content (blogs) on a regular basis, drive relevant traffic to these pieces of content, and as your web traffic grows, you monetize this traffic.

You can monetize your blog traffic through various strategies such as affiliate marketing, ad partnerships, offering coaching services, pay walling some of your most valuable content (membership sites), or even selling your own products.

Blogging is a great business model that has tons of advantages—such as the ability to create a successful brand (TechCrunch, started a blog and is now a successful brand, so is the Huffpost and various other blogs)—and massive passive income potential. In fact, by concentrating on blogging alone, you can create a business that generates 6-figures in passive income each month. Some blogs such as smartblogger.com generate $60,000+ in passive income each month.

Blogging For Income: A Quick Getting Started Guide

Here are the steps you need to take to implement this business model to generate a 6-figure passive income that allows you to create the lifestyle of your dreams.

Step 1

To create a successful blog that generates a 6-figure passive income month after month, you must choose your niche carefully; a niche is simply the topic of your blog.

Your blog should be on an interesting topic that is personally interesting—you will need to write content for the blog {you can outsource this service to capable freelancers and that has a broad online audience or appeal.

The best way to choose a niche for your blog is to think about what you would like to learn, ideas that interest you, and whether they are others online who have similar questions or interests.

Create a general list of ideas you would like to blog about and then whittle the list down to 1-3 ideas. This resource page has a list of blog niches you can use for inspiration purposes:100 Blog Niches.

Step 2

After choosing an interest blog topic, one that also has great online appeal, the next step is to buy a relevant domain name and web hosting.

Your domain name can be the name of your blog or business; for instance, Routerreviews.com would be a great domain and business name for a blog (or online business) concentrated on writing and publishing honest/genuine router review.

On hosting, you can go the semi-hosted or self-hosted route; opt for the self-hosted route because it gives you customizability and functionality. You can get web hosting for as little as $3 per month.

If you don't want to get lost in the sea of web hosting possibilities Bluehost * is a great option easy to set up and with good prices.

Step 3

Once your blog is up and running, commit to publishing blogs often—2-5 times a week should be ideal—because publishing relevant and helpful, search optimized content is one part of the multi-strategy approach that will help you drive more traffic to your blog and monetize this traffic into a passive income.

Step 4

The fourth step is to market the blog as the success of your blog as an income-generating tool depends on it.

How effectively you manage to market your blog will depend on your online marketing and SEO skill level, as well as your adeptness at learning and internalizing new concepts.

While this is not an exhaustive list, the following tips should help you market your blog once you create it, and scale the blog to a point where it generates passive income from various source streams.

Blogging Success Tips

Once you get started with blogging, skyrocket your chances of success and ability to scale by implementing the following tips:

Your content is the pillar

To serve your blog audience effectively enough to keep them coming back to your blog day after day and bringing along their friends, you need to create content; a common comment in the blogosphere is that content is king!

Here, the only secret to success is to create valuable content. To reiterate, the value you provide within your chosen industry/niche significantly influences how much traffic your blog generates and eventually, how much income your blog generates in passive income.

Blogs that earn a consistent, passive income each month are those that provide their target audience access to an immense amount of value in terms of content disseminated through various mediums: YouTube Videos, blogs, tutorials, reviews, podcasts, etc.

Create an effective content strategy, one that allows you to create viral content and check/track the effectiveness of your content marketing plan. As mentioned, you can write the content yourself, or, if you want to grow and scale rapidly, you can use iWriter, Upwork, and the many other gig economy platforms to contract capable freelance writers, which will allow you more time to market and grow your blog rapidly.

As a necessity, learn SEO

We have mentioned SEO severally throughout this guide. This is because with online businesses and most work from home opportunities, your discoverability, i.e., to mean how visible your business or content is, determines the level of attention you generate.

SEO should be an integral part of your online marketing strategy, and you should experiment with as many SEO marketing and optimization strategies as you can so that you can learn what works and does not work for you, as well as skyrocket your traffic and therefore your revenue-and-scalability potential.

With learning SEO as fast as possible so that you can use the residual knowledge to drive more traffic to your blog and then monetize this blog traffic into a 6-figure business that generates a passive income, the internet is your best friend.

Use Google Search as partner that helps you learn about SEO elements such as:

Keyword research
How to write amazing blog posts
How to use SEO to drive more traffic to your blog, etc.

Learning SEO is a necessity because how effectively you do it will determine the visibility of your blog on search and general online space, which will then influence how much traffic your blog attracts. The more traffic you attract, the more your blog is likely to earn—provided you monetize it appropriately.

Use various monetization strategies

The best thing about a blog as a vehicle you can use to generate a 6-figure passive income is that although it takes a while and a lot of work to get a blog to a point where it has enough traction to generate a steady and healthy stream of traffic, you can monetize a blog in various ways.

For example, once you use the tips illustrated in this guide to create a successful blog that, say, generates 50,000 in monthly traffic, you can monetize this traffic using affiliate marketing, sponsored advertisements, creating and selling your own products, pay walling some of your content—making part of your blog content accessible to members only—email marketing, etc.

You can learn more about the various ways to monetize a blog from the following resource pages.

https://trafficsalesandprofit.com/how-to-scale-your-blog-business/

https://www.quicksprout.com/5-stages-of-blog-growth-and-traffic-tactics/

Here, we shall concentrate on affiliate marketing and selling information products because they are the easiest to implement and perhaps the most lucrative. Both make up a large portion of the income generated by most, if not all, successful blogs.

A Basic Introduction to Affiliate Marketing

In affiliate marketing, you promote/market other people's products and services using a specially created link called an affiliate link. For your marketing efforts, when the audiences you market to use your link to purchase a product you are recommending or marketing, the vendor/business credits a pre-decided percentage of the sale price to you as an affiliate commission.

Affiliate marketing is great as a tool you can use to create a work from home business that generates a 6-figure income because among other things, it affords you flexibility and a million chances to recommend/market something. Think of it as follows:
Every sentence or paragraph you write for your blogs is a chance you can (or cannot) choose to use to market a product by twining relevant affiliate links into your content always with the intention to be of immense value to your audiences. Moreover, a single blogpost can have more than one affiliate link—as long as you openly disclose an affiliate association—and recommend more than one product or service. This makes the earning potential here exponential especially if you successfully create a traffic-generating, popular blog.

Some popular blogs such as the Huffpost generate upwards of $45+ million each month, a large percentage of which comes from affiliate marketing and informational products.

To create a monthly income from affiliate marketing, the most important concept you need to keep in mind is that your recommendations should be genuine and aimed at helping your target audiences achieve whatever need has brought them to your page or website. Ethical affiliate marketing, which includes disclosing an affiliate relationship and recommending products you would be willing to stand by, is the way to win the game.

Secondly, write content that has audience appeal. As a source of passive income, affiliate marketing works best when coupled with an effective content creating strategy and viral content. Strive to offer your niche audience more value than anyone within your space does by creating the best, most detailed blog posts and content in different formats. By doing this, you will also have many chances to integrate relevant affiliate links into your valuable content.

In addition to the above, and any other affiliate marketing knowledge you may learn outside this book, only work with reputable affiliate programs such as [ClickBank](#)*, ShareASale, and other industry-trusted independent affiliate marketing channels.

A Brief Introduction to Selling Informational Products

Informational products are digital products such as eBooks, online courses, membership sites, teardown and templates, theme packages, plugins, cheat sheets, webinars, and most other forms of digital products.

With this monetization strategy/business model, you spend time creating a valuable downloadable product, and once you complete the creation process, you simply sell the same product to a thousand different people—you sell a digital product to as many people as possible.

The passive income-potency within selling informational products online comes from the fact that you create a product once and resell it multiple times, and the fact that you can create a varied portfolio of profitable digital products. For instance, you can get into eBook publishing by outsourcing the writing and cover creation process to good freelancers; at the same time, you could be getting ready to create and publish an online course.

The other great thing about this business model is that most of the online marketing strategies we have discussed throughout this guide—such as choosing a great product or niche, mastering SEO, networking, etc.,—will prove very effective here too.

Like affiliate marketing, informational products have exponential potential to turn into businesses that generate a great Passive income business. Here is an example, if you have two eBooks priced at $10 each, and you sell 100 of these eBooks per month, it amounts to $1,000 or more per month.

If you couple this with two online courses priced at $15 and you sell 50 instances of this course each month, it is $1500 in passive income or a combined total of $2500 each month. You can replicate this across different informational products to create a thriving home business that allows you to create the lifestyle you dream of, one rich in financial and time freedom and independence.

If you find this path suits you K Money Mastery * from Stefan James is an awesome course that teaches you a step by step self publishing method for selling Books in Amazon that can get you started with in a month.

To achieve success and scale an informational products business, create products that have market appeal, market them like your income depends on it—it does—network, and offer superior customer support so that you can create a brandable, follow-worthy business.

If you implement these ideas diligently, you should be able to create a thriving online business that earns a steady passive income each month. Worth mentioning is that most passive income streams usually start out active. For instance, writing, blogging, and affiliate marketing usually start out as active income streams since you have to dedicate time and energy to establishing them.

With the above mentioned, implemented with some fore thought and planning, all the business models discussed in this guide have the potential to become passive (or semi-passive) businesses that generate a six-figure passive income.

Conclusion

We have come to the end of the book. Thank you for reading and congratulations for reading until the end.

Take what you have learned from it, implement it, and keep implementing and learning until you have several streams of well-established, location-independent, work-from-home online businesses that generate a 6-figure income each month.

Finally if you found the book valuable, I will appreciate you leave an honest review on Amazon, so others can also find the book.

Leave your Review Here

Bonus:Get our next books FREE

We have a reviewers list which we send our books for free before being published.
They enjoy the ebook beforehand, we only expect to get an honest review from the in return.

Join Here

Thank you and good luck!

Michael Cobble - Digital Media Life

www.ingramcontent.com/pod-product-compliance
Lightning Source LLC
Chambersburg PA
CBHW070845220526
45466CB00002B/893